MW00445011

Health, Healing, and Wholeness

Thank you, Mrs. Pat, for the work you do to bring hope to cancer patients. May you experience God's Health, Healing, & Wholeness every day.

Blessings,
Tracy Crump

Health, Healing, and Wholeness

DEVOTIONS OF HOPE
IN THE MIDST OF ILLNESS

TRACY CRUMP

CrossLink Publishing

CrossLink Publishing
1601 Mt. Rushmore Rd, STE 3288
Rapid City, SD 57702

Health, Healing, and Wholeness/Crump —1st ed.
ISBN 978-1-63357-328-4
Library of Congress Control Number: 2020938510
First edition: 10 9 8 7 6 5 4 3 2 1

Published in association with Cyle Young of C.Y.L.E. (Cyle Young Literary Elite, LLC), a literary agency.
Cover design by The Dragomir Group

This book is not intended as a substitute for the medical advice of physicians. The reader should regularly consult a physician in matters relating to his/her health, particularly with respect to any symptoms that may require diagnosis or medical attention.

Stories contained within this book are from the author's memory of events and conversations. In order to maintain patients' anonymity, she has occassionally changed the names of individuals and places.

Praise for *Health, Healing, and Wholeness*

Most devotional books come across as sweet-but-empty of content. By contrast, ICU nurse Tracy Crump interacted with patients in their most critical moments. Not only did she minister to them, but they, in turn, enriched her life. With compassion, she shares those powerful experiences with readers.

—**Cecil Murphey**, best-selling author of *90 Minutes in Heaven* with Don Piper and author of 140 books, including *When Someone You Love No Longer Remembers*

Tracy uses real-life accounts of people as a springboard to direct our thoughts to specific biblical truths. She explains God's Word and provides hope and encouragement for the reader. The prayers at the end of each devotional help guide your thoughts and give you a starting point for your own prayers. This devotional will be a great gift for any Christ-follower.

—**Shirley Crowder**, award-winning author of devotional books and books on prayer

Tracy Crump has penned a book that will touch your heart. As you read the stories, you will see God working in each situation, reminding us He will never leave us alone and will always bring us through whatever situation we encounter. Through the pages you will feel God's love.

—**Susan Reichert**, cofounder and former editor in chief of *Southern Writers Magazine*

Tracy Crump's actual accounts of her patients' healing, both physical and spiritual, bring inspiration, encouragement, and joy. Each devotion led me to think about my own faith, learn the lessons Tracy learned from her experiences, and pray along with her. The Scripture verses offer a renewed appreciation of God's presence and care and the reminder that in our most troubled times there is love, help, and hope.

—**Yvonne Lehman**, author of 59 novels and 15 Divine Moments books, founder of Blue Ridge Mountains Christian Writers Conference

Reading *Health, Healing and Wholeness: Devotions of Hope in the Midst of Illness* is like drinking from a cool stream on a long hike. Tracy's words revive a weary soul and refresh a tired heart. I devoured this book in one sitting, and I look forward to reading it again and again.

—**Josie Siler**, award-winning writer and vice president of Broken but Priceless Ministries

Tracy Crump's stories and spiritual insights tug at the heart and inspire hope in the God who can heal body and soul.

—**Katy Kauffman**, cofounder of Lighthouse Bible Studies and editor of *Refresh Bible Study Magazine*

Health, Healing, and Wholeness gives an intimate glimpse into the lives of those going through a personal health crisis. Your heart will feel an immediate tug of compassion, joy, and hope as Tracy Crump blends personal life experiences with spiritual truths. These personal stories will inspire hope in the hearts of all who read.

—**Theresa Rowe**, TV host of *Shaped by Faith with Theresa Rowe*, author of *Shaped by Faith: 10 Secrets to Strengthening Your Body & Soul*

Simple yet thought provoking. Tender yet convicting. Tracy Crump crafts a timeless devotional to help us focus on the Giver of health. Well-done and memorable, these devotions guarantee the Word of God will not only apply to your life but remain as a daily reminder of God's love.

—**Cindy K. Sproles**, best-selling author and cofounder, Christian Devotions Ministries

Our world needs more compassion and empathy, and Tracy Crump delivers both in *Health, Healing, and Wholeness*. My heart melted, broke, and soared reading story after story of small victories through major trials. Tracy wraps up each testimony by expertly applying God's Word to each circumstance and lesson. This is a book you'll want to turn to time and again to remember how much God loves us and how we can always trust Him, even through difficult circumstances.

—**Bethany Jett**, award-winning author of *Platinum Faith*

Having been through my own health crises on more than one occasion, I can vouch that this book would have encouraged me not only to "hang in there" but also to lean into the Lord. This book is not just theory—the stories the author shares are from her own life and experiences, from people she has known and touched. The stories do not all have happy-ever-after endings, which makes them all the more relevant, but they all conclude with the clear message: my health, healing, and wholeness come from God, who is always in control.

—**Shirley Corder**, author of *Strength Renewed: Meditations for Your Journey through Breast Cancer*

Drawing from the power of her sharp storytelling skills, Tracy Crump has assembled an encouraging and inspiring devotional that points us to the One who is our source of peace and comfort. Partnering each story with the truth of Scripture and a prayer, each devotional delivers on the promise of hope within its pages. *Health, Healing and Wholeness: Devotions of Hope in the Midst of Illness* is sure to encourage anyone who reads it!

—**Victoria Duerstock**, speaker, coach and author of multiple books including *Advent Devotions & Christmas Crafts for Families,* Skyhorse Publishing, 2020

In *Health, Healing, and Wholeness*, author Tracy Crump has provided a lifeline for those in the midst of illness. Her stories of encouragement not only give hope but point us to the ultimate Healer. This is a book I'll give as a gift over and over again.

—**Edie Melson**, award-winning author and director of the Blue Ridge Mountains Christian Writers Conference

When I served as a professional hospital chaplain, I met many devout believers who faced a health crisis. In the midst of any battle for our health, we are desperately seeking words of comfort, encouragement, and hope. Tracy Crump provides these precious words in her book, *Health, Healing, and Wholeness: Devotions of Hope in the Midst of Illness.* This book will be a source of strength for patients and their families as they walk through the unique challenges of health and healing.

—**Dr. Craig von Buseck**, Inspiration Ministries

This book is dedicated to all those who face a health crisis, whether as a patient or caregiver. When medical science has no answers, God is still your hope and healer.

Contents

Acknowledgments

I hesitated to include an acknowledgments page for fear I would leave out someone, which no doubt I have. So many people have invested in my writing journey, and I am grateful for you all.

Marylane Wade Koch, my writing partner and co-director of Write Life Workshops, encouraged me to submit my first story to a Chicken Soup for the Soul book about nurses and started a long line of acceptances.

Kathy Carlton Willis invited me to join her online critique group and coached me in many areas. I now lead the KCW Mentoring Group and couldn't do without them. Members, both past and present, have challenged me to hone and polish my work.

Ed Gilbreath, editor of *Today's Christian*, published my first article and patiently held my hand through the process. Cecil Murphey, every writer's friend, offered encouragement and insight along the way.

Most recently, my Facebook launch group—Tracy's Team—engaged in some lively discussions about Bible versions and offered input on back cover content. You're the best!

Special thanks to Rhonda Dragomir of The Dragomir Group, who not only provided her expertise for editing and cover design but acted as a stalwart support through my ups and downs. I appreciate you more than you know.

Thank you to Cyle Young and Bethany Morehead (Cyle Young Literary Elite), who paved the way for this book to be published, and to Rick Bates and his expert team at CrossLink Publishing, whose skill and expertise turned words on a page into a book.

I can't forget my family: Stan, my husband of more than forty years, and our sons and their families—Brian, Courtney, Bennett, and Ayla and Jeremy, Lindsey, Nellie, and Matthew. I love you!

And most of all, thank you, Jesus—the rock on which we all stand.

Introduction

P ain and illness, caregiving and grief often overwhelm us, whether they touch our own lives or those of our family and friends. We may be tempted to cry out to God, "Don't You care if we drown?" just as the disciples did when a storm threatened to capsize their boat (Mark 4:38 NIV). Knowing that the same Christ who calmed the sea stands ready to "[take] up our infirmities and [bear] our diseases" (Matthew 8:17 NIV) enables us to make it through another day. By leaning on Jesus, we find strength to face even the worst of illnesses.

In my work as an intensive care nurse, I watched God perform miracles when everyone else had given up. While we don't always experience physical healing in this life, we can find hope in Jesus no matter what our situation. Regardless of how things appear now, we can look forward to a glorious future with anticipation and joy in the return of our Savior when "the Sun of Righteousness will rise with healing in his wings" (Malachi 4:2 NLT).

I pray that you find comfort, encouragement, and peace in these devotions. I take my task seriously to stay true to God's Word, believing the goal of a devotional book is to point readers back to Scripture. God's Word alone brings hope.

Beloved, I pray that all may go well with you and that you may be in good health, as it goes well with your soul.

— 3 John 2 —

In His Hands

Winter weather had trapped eighteen-month-old Emily inside for days. When the next morning dawned cold and clear, her mother bundled the toddler into a stroller and set out for a walk along their country lane. As they topped a hill, sun glinting off a patch of snow blinded a driver coming from the other direction, and he struck the stroller. The impact sent Emily flying thirty feet where she landed on her head.

When she arrived at our hospital, Emily's pupils were fixed and dilated. Doctors rushed her to surgery to relieve pressure in her skull, but they could do little more. One neurosurgeon later described the right half of her brain as "oatmeal." His prognosis? "She'll never walk or talk again." In ICU, where I cared for her, Emily rebounded from one crisis only to face another as her mother's hope waned. Eventually, Emily became stable enough to transfer to the pediatric floor, and I never expected to hear anything more about my beautiful little patient.

Two weeks later, another nurse gave me surprising news: Emily was being discharged. Not only that, but she had reached for her mother, calling her "mama," and asked for "wata." The next day, she walked into her mother's arms.

The Bible relates many accounts of Jesus' healing miracles—from restoring a man's withered hand (Luke 6:6-10) to raising a little girl from the dead (Mark 5:22-24, 35-42). Why then are we incredulous when God heals people today? Many times, He works through medical professionals, but doctors do not have control over life and death and can't predict the outcome of every situation. They can be just as surprised—and thrilled—as we are when God chooses to work contrary to expectations.

God does not guarantee a miracle in every health crisis, but Emily taught me that no one is beyond hope. We seek good medical care, but we place our faith and trust in God, wisely remembering that our times are in His hands (Psalm 31:15). The results rest with Him alone.

Prayer
Father, only You hold my life in Your hands. Whether You choose to work a healing miracle or not, I know You love me and have my best interests in mind. Whatever happens, I praise Your holy name. Amen.

Lord, by such things people live; and my spirit finds life in them too. You restored me to health and let me live.

— Isaiah 38:16 NIV —

Touch of Compassion

Because of the LORD's great love we are not con-
sumed, for his compassions never fail.
— Lamentations 3:22 NIV —

With trembling white-stockinged legs, I took a deep breath and entered the hospital room of my very first patient as a student nurse. Mrs. Robbins, a frail eighty-seven-year-old with congestive heart failure, smiled when I said I was there to give her a bath. Bless her, she didn't know what she was in for.

After filling a basin with water just the right temperature, I folded the washcloth the way they'd taught us in class so the cold ends wouldn't drag across my patient's skin. I proceeded to wash, rinse, and dry one body part after another, rewarm the water, hold a straw so she could drink a cup of orange juice, rewarm the water, hold an emesis basin so she could redeposit the orange juice, rewarm the water, cover her when the doctor came in for a fifteen-minute talk, rewarm the water, finish bathing her, change the bed, apply lotion to her legs, and brush her sparse, white hair. Whew! Two hours later, my instructor and the other student nurses had returned to the dorm while I still tidied up. About to take my leave, I remembered the final component of a "complete" bed bath.

"Mrs. Robbins, would you like a backrub?" I asked.

"Is it included?" When I nodded, she said, "Give me the works!" Her contented sighs made the whole morning worthwhile.

Nothing comforts and connects like a compassionate touch. A pat, hug, stroke, or just a hand on the shoulder conveys love like words can never do. Jesus became God's hand on earth, and touch characterized His ministry. Matthew recorded many of Christ's miracles in which Jesus used touch to heal a leper (8:3), relieve fever (8:15), and restore sight (9:29, 20:34). After His resurrection, Jesus turned around and invited His disciples to touch Him, to feel the nail-pierced hands that freed them from sin (Luke 24:39).

Physical touch is important, but it's Jesus' spiritual touch that makes us whole. By His wounds we are healed (1 Peter 2:24), and once He has touched us, we will never be the same again. That's the true touch of compassion.

Prayer
Lord, sometimes I just need a touch from You. Please show me You are walking through this valley with me. Amen.

*That which was from the beginning, which we have
heard, which we have seen with our eyes, which we
have looked at and our hands have touched—this we
proclaim concerning the Word of life.*
— *1 John 1:1 NIV* —

A Blessed Life

*Now to him who is able to do immeasurably more
than all we ask or imagine, according to his power
that is at work within us, to him be glory in the
church and in Christ Jesus throughout all generations,
for ever and ever! Amen.*
— Ephesians 3:20-21 NIV —

Jenny struggled to breathe. Clubbed fingers and the bluish cast to her skin bespoke a lifetime battle with heart disease. Scars crisscrossed her chest, badges of valor from cardiac surgeries too numerous to count. Born with tetralogy of Fallot, a rare congenital disorder that causes four major heart defects, her condition was so severe doctors did not expect her to survive childhood. When she did, they discouraged her from having children with warnings that her heart was too weak to support a pregnancy.

Jenny was thirty-seven when I met her, and she had a twelve-year-old daughter who made her struggles worth enduring. "I've already lived longer than the doctors said I would," she whispered between gasping breaths. "My daughter is older than they thought I would ever be. I'm so grateful for my life."

No stranger to intensive care, she'd been admitted with heart failure. Doctors told her they could do little else for her. But God had already done so much more than the doctors could ever dream of doing.

While none of us would choose to begin life with a weak heart, God's ways are not our ways nor His thoughts our thoughts (Isaiah 55:8). He has plans for us we know nothing about. Often the difference between living a miserable life focused on illness and a blessed life rich in God's glory is remembering the benefits God has heaped upon us in so many other ways (Job 10:12). Not that it's easy to do when pain, weakness, and fear dog our steps. What then? Like Jenny, we can live in gratitude for what God has already done for us and what He will do, "according to his power that is at work within us" (Ephesians 3:20 NIV).

With medication adjustments and support therapy, Jenny returned home. I don't know how much longer she lived, but I have no doubt she was grateful for every minute.

Prayer
Lord, forgive me when I complain about my problems and forget to acknowledge all You have done in my life. You give me so much to be thankful for if I will only look for it. Amen.

Praise the LORD, my soul; all my inmost being, praise his holy name. Praise the LORD, my soul, and forget not all his benefits.
— *Psalm 103:1-2 NIV* —

Heaven-Sent Aid

Yet it was kind of you to share my trouble . . . Even
in Thessalonica you sent me help for my needs once
and again.
— Philippians 4:14,16 —

Rushed to the hospital with crushing chest pain, Stephen underwent an emergency quadruple by-pass. In the midst of the operation, doctors made an alarming discovery—a dangerous aneurism ballooned from Stephen's aorta, the largest artery in the body. He was too unstable for prolonged surgery, so the repair would require a second operation.

Unfortunately, Stephen had recently changed jobs and was eleven days away from having insurance. Before considering a second surgery date, the hospital informed him they would require a deposit, and the surgeon insisted on payment for the first surgery. The cardiologist also asked for money, and Stephen simply didn't have it. As a former nurse, I knew an aortic aneurysm left untreated is a ticking time bomb. Eventually it will rupture and cost the patient his life. This wasn't something that could wait.

Three other families joined mine to race against the clock and help provide for Stephen's need. We held a benefit and collected more than we'd dreamed of making but fell far short of the amount needed to pay for surgery. However, when the surgeon heard about the fundraiser, he said, "If you have that kind of backing from the community, I'm not worried about getting my fee."

From Leviticus (19:18) through James (2:8), the Bible tells us to love our neighbors as ourselves, and Jesus gives us the perfect example in His parable of the good Samaritan (Luke 10:30-37). When we answer the call to help someone else, we deliver the blessing God sends, whether through our financial gifts or offers of meals, rides to the doctor, or a good house cleaning. At the same time, we're blessed for our willingness to join in God's provision (Acts 20:35).

What if we are the ones who find ourselves in the position of needing help, just as Paul did in Thessalonica? When we graciously accept and receive God's abundant gifts through others, we allow them to be a blessing.

God not only saw Stephen through successful aneurysm surgery but brought neighbors alongside to meet his need. Stephen returned home to his family, free of an impending death sentence and fortified by God's provision.

Prayer
Father, show me where I can help those in need. At the same time, let me humbly accept the gifts You send through my loving neighbors. Amen.

Every good gift and every perfect gift is from above,
coming down from the Father of lights, with whom
there is no variation or shadow due to change.
— James 1:17 —

A Divine Answer

"So I have been allotted months of futility, and nights of misery have been assigned to me. When I lie down I think, 'How long before I get up?' The night drags on, and I toss and turn until dawn."
— *Job 7:3-4 NIV* —

My vibrant mother's mental state was rapidly declining. A neurologist did a cursory exam and diagnosed her with dementia, but that didn't explain her odd motor symptoms. Within three months, her memory was almost nil, and she could no longer walk or speak more than one or two words at a time. Something else was wrong. What?

During the day, I took her from one specialist to another. At night, I tossed and turned, alternately begging God for answers and trying to reason out the problem on my own. *This is stupid*, I told myself as the clock ticked away hours with fruitless worrying. Yet in that dreamlike stage between consciousness and sleep, I couldn't keep my thoughts from running amok.

After weeks of little sleep, I finally gave up, exhausted. *Lord, there's nothing more I can do*, I prayed. *Please forgive me for trying to play god.* As I drifted off to sleep, I remembered a friend whose father had symptoms similar to Mom's. What was his diagnosis? The words floated into my mind. Normal pressure hydrocephalus. Once I let go, God gave me the answer I had tried so hard to discern on my own.

The Creator of the universe holds the solution to all our dilemmas, but pride sometimes leads us to depend on earthly wisdom. Then we find ourselves in King David's position when he asked, "How long must I wrestle with my thoughts and day after day have sorrow in my heart?" (Psalm 13:2 NIV). Only by putting ourselves completely in God's hands—by submitting to Him in all our ways (Proverbs 3:6)—can we hear His voice.

Mom had a shunt inserted to drain fluid that had built up in her brain and caused her symptoms. Three days later, her memory returned, and she could carry on a conversation. What a joy to have my mother back!

I can reason things out all day long, but in the end, I'm still relying on my limited human abilities. Next time I face a health crisis, I'll let go of my own understanding and look first to the One who holds all the answers.

Prayer
Father, forgive me for relying on myself when it's You and Your wisdom I need. Amen.

If any of you lacks wisdom, you should ask God,
who gives generously to all without finding fault, and
it will be given to you.
— James 1:5 NIV —

Our Lifeline

Let us then with confidence draw near to the throne
of grace, that we may receive mercy and find grace to
help in time of need.
— *Hebrews 4:16* —

octors questioned whether Angela's vague symptoms were psychosomatic—until she stopped breathing. They put the 26-year-old on a ventilator and rushed her to ICU where she was later diagnosed with Guillian-Barré Syndrome—a progressive, but usually temporary, condition. Creeping relentlessly up her body, the syndrome robbed Angela of the ability to move her hands, nod her head, and mouth words until all she could do was blink: one for yes and two for no. It became her sole means of communication. Then one day, she lost even that.

For weeks, Angela remained trapped in limbo. Though her body refused to respond to even the simplest command, that didn't mean she couldn't hear, but she needed more than "I'm going to change your gown now." Instead, I described the weather outside her windowless room, told her my plans for Christmas, and regaled her with the antics of my new puppy. I offered her a lifeline to the world she could not reach.

God offers us the same lifeline. Through prayer, we connect with a world we can neither see nor touch, one where the ruler of the universe dwells. He makes a way for us to communicate through His Son, our "great high priest," who empathizes with our weaknesses (Hebrews 4:14), and through the Holy Spirit, who intercedes for us when we don't even know what to pray (Romans 8:26). We can tell Him our deepest hurts and most urgent needs. And God promises to listen no matter when we pray (Psalm 55:17). Though we're trapped for now in this world, God wants to keep the lifeline of communication open.

Angela eventually regained use of her muscles and later told me she remembered my voice from our one-sided "conversations." She'd latched on to the thread formed between us, a thread that grew into a lifeline the more I talked to her. We, too, can strengthen our bond with God the more we talk to Him in prayer. Perhaps when Paul admonished the Thessalonians to "pray without ceasing" (1 Thessalonians 5:17), he had a lifeline of constant communication in mind.

Prayer
Lord, I commit now to come to You in prayer throughout the day, both speaking to You and listening for Your voice. I want to keep my lifeline strong. Amen.

*Rejoice in hope, be patient in tribulation, be constant
in prayer.*
— *Romans 12:12* —-

Now That's Love

*Greater love has no one than this: to lay down one's
life for one's friends.*
— John 15:13 NIV —

All grandchildren are perfect, of course, but our little grandson Bennett was an exceptionally easy baby. He slept through the night at a few weeks old and rarely fussed. But when he turned three months, he began kicking and screaming whenever he was fed. The pediatrician soon identified the problem. Bennett's little body couldn't process milk protein. A special formula the doctor prescribed didn't eliminate his symptoms, and an alternate formula came with an exorbitant price tag.

My daughter-in-law Courtney decided to continue breast-feeding, but that meant she had to cut not only dairy but also soy products from her own diet. Even a single slip— she once ate a frozen fruit bar not realizing it contained dairy—meant several wakeful nights with a cramping baby. Courtney learned to read every food label and question servers at restaurants before ordering. And though she wouldn't breast-feed forever, her research showed she might experience symptoms herself when she reintroduced dairy and soy to her diet. Yet she chose the risk for Bennett's sake.

Thanks to his mom, Bennett has grown into a healthy pre-schooler who can eat some dairy with no ill effects.

As my ninety-nine-year-old mother-in-law said of Courtney's sacrifice, "Now that's love."

Love manifests itself in many ways, the most commendable being self-sacrifice. Nevertheless, what parents do for their children can't compare with what God did for us. In fact, the gospel can be summed up in one beautiful verse: "For God so loved the world that he gave his one and only Son, that whoever believes in him shall not perish but have eternal life" (John 3:16 NIV). How do we respond to such love? As the psalmist said, "What shall I return to the LORD for all his goodness to me? I will lift up the cup of salvation and call on the name of the LORD" (Psalm 116:12-13 NIV).

Shortly after Bennett was born, Courtney said, "I would literally lie down on train tracks for him." Many parents feel the same way. But God didn't sacrifice *for* His Son. He sacrificed His Son *for us*. Jesus' death on the cross and our acceptance of that gift freed us from sin's hold, and "by his wounds we are healed" (Isaiah 53:5 NIV).

Now that's love!

Prayer
Heavenly Father, thank You for the sacrificial gift of Your Son who died for me on the cross. Let me never take Your love for granted. Amen.

*God demonstrates his own love for us in this: While
we were still sinners, Christ died for us.*
— Romans 5:8 NIV —

Heal Me, Lord!

Heal me, O Lord, and I shall be healed; save me,
and I shall be saved, for you are my praise.
— Jeremiah 17:14 —

Mary Dee's journey started one autumn with a bad cold—or so she thought. Her cough dragged on for weeks and then months. Various doctors treated her for bronchitis or the flu while she progressively worsened. Rebounding a little in February, Mary Dee and her husband, Terry, joined some friends for a fishing trip. By the time they returned home, she could hardly put one foot in front of the other. After tests revealed she had not only a high white cell count but an alarmingly low platelet count, the doctor ordered her to the ER, "Now!"

Pulmonologists, oncologists, and infectious disease doctors converged upon her. They considered diagnoses such as tuberculosis and pneumonia, all the while pumping her full of antibiotics. Mary Dee continued to decline. Doctors ordered x-rays, CT scans, and bloodwork but still could not determine what was wrong. They gave her a 20 percent chance of survival. In the meantime, infusions couldn't keep up with her platelet loss. Finally, a bone marrow biopsy showed she had contracted histoplasmosis, a common fungal infection.

It had spread throughout her body and begun attacking her other organs.

In all, Mary Dee spent five weeks in the hospital—three of those in ICU—and ten days on a ventilator. As frustrating and harrowing as her experience was, her faith and that of her husband never wavered. She knew God would heal her, whether in this world or the next.

I often think of Job when I hear a story like Mary Dee's, not only because of the trials she experienced but because she never blamed God (Job 1:21-22). Without doubt, the Lord pulled her through, yet He did even more by using Terry to witness online with prayer and Scripture during his wife's hospital stay (Acts 20:24). As a result, many people united to pray. They were encouraged to look up rather than look to the world for strength, comfort, and healing. God brought good from what was one of the worst times in Mary Dee's life (Romans 8:28).

But then, that's what God is best at doing.

Prayer
Father, thank You for healing me, whether in this world or the next, and strengthening me through my trials. Amen.

Count it all joy, my brothers, when you meet trials of various kinds, for you know that the testing of your faith produces steadfastness. And let steadfastness have its full effect, that you may be perfect and complete, lacking in nothing.
— *James 1:2-4* —

Consequences

Or do you not know that your body is a temple of the
Holy Spirit within you, whom you have from God?
You are not your own, for you were bought with a
price. So glorify God in your body.
— 1 Corinthians 6:19-20 —

My grandmother, the youngest of fifteen children, grew up the daughter of penniless farmers in Oklahoma. She earned a reputation as the family's wild child and made poor choices throughout her lifetime, some of which came with dire consequences. A talented singer and guitarist, she forfeited a career in music for alcohol and men. Later, alcoholism caused her to lose many things, including jobs and her driver's license.

However, her tobacco habit came with the highest price. As a child, I often watched her roll her own unfiltered cigarettes. She smoked them for forty years, and they eventually led to cancer. Years of drinking alcohol and not eating properly had weakened her, compounding her illness.

Bad choices often lead to sin, and sin—any sin—carries a high price. The apostle Paul told the Romans that "the wages of sin is death." Then he offered hope by adding "but the free gift of God is eternal life in Christ Jesus our Lord"

(Romans 6:23). Hallelujah! God does not treat us as we deserve, unlike our bodies. Instead, He gives us the means to erase all our transgressions by becoming His child through faith in Jesus Christ. God says, "I am he who blots out your transgressions for my own sake, and I will not remember your sins" (Isaiah 43:25).

Might we still face consequences from poor choices while on this earth? Unfortunately, yes. God, through His mercy, may heal us physically. Or He may not. Regardless, we can find complete spiritual healing through Jesus. Revelation 21:4 tells us: "[God] will wipe away every tear from their eyes, and death shall be no more, neither shall there be mourning, nor crying, nor pain anymore, for the former things have passed away." Those are the results of finding spiritual health at any age. And those are consequences I can live with.

Prayer
Father, please help me make choices that honor You with my body, even when I've made poor choices in the past. I praise You for the healing You bring. Amen.

As far as the east is from the west, so far does he remove our transgressions from us. As a father shows compassion to his children, so the LORD shows compassion to those who fear him.

— Psalm 103:12-13 —

No Favorites

So Peter opened his mouth and said: "Truly I understand that God shows no partiality, but in every nation anyone who fears him and does what is right is acceptable to him."
— Acts 10:34-35 —

When I was in nursing school, I happened to rotate through the coronary care unit while Vernon Presley, Elvis Presley's father, was a patient there. Yes, *that* Elvis Presley. I'm ashamed to say my friends and I each found a reason to go into Mr. Presley's room—to check his IV, take vital signs, or offer him some water, of course. This poor man wasn't even famous, but we all found it exciting to be near someone who was near someone famous.

How silly. Our patient was just human. When cholesterol lined his arteries, he became ill as any of us would. Now, both he *and* his famous son are gone.

Singers, movie stars, sports figures—we may hold many well-known people in high regard simply because they display a talent or achieve something remarkable. Unlike us, God does not play favorites (Romans 2:11). Fame will not get anyone into heaven (John 3:3, Titus 3:5).

Poor Job realized this even at his lowest point. Anticipating his impending death, he reminded his detractors that God "shows no partiality to princes, nor regards the rich more than the poor" since He made them all. "In a moment they die; at midnight the people are shaken and pass away, and the mighty are taken away by no human hand" (Job 34:19-20).

Depressing? Some may think so, but I find this quite encouraging. When my time comes, it won't matter how much money, education, or fame I possess—or lack. We all stand equal before God. Jesus' sacrifice covers everyone who believes.

What a relief! Elvis may be part of the angelic choir, but with a voice like mine, I'm glad my salvation doesn't depend on singing ability.

Prayer
Lord, nothing I do could ever live up to Your standards. Thank You that You saved me by grace though faith alone that I may live eternally with You. Amen.

For the Scripture says, "Everyone who believes in him will not be put to shame." For there is no distinction between Jew and Greek; for the same Lord is Lord of all, bestowing his riches on all who call on him. For "everyone who calls on the name of the Lord will be saved."

— Romans 10:11-13 —

Capable Hands

"For as the Father raises the dead and gives them life,
so also the Son gives life to whom he will."
— John 5:21 —

When surgery techs rolled Mr. Hanson into intensive care, he wore the same terror-stricken look of most of our coronary artery bypass patients. Though open-heart surgery is no breeze, most patients did quite well and transferred to the floor within three or four days. Nevertheless, I understood the fear associated with such a serious operation. I untangled Mr. Hanson's mass of tubes and lines and tried to reassure him that he was doing fine. Still, he watched my every move.

Later in the night, he developed atrial fibrillation, an irregular heartbeat not uncommon in bypass patients. I acted quickly, calling his doctor and giving him the appropriate medication. He soon converted to a normal rhythm. By the way he grabbed my hand and thanked me over and over, you would have thought I'd raised him from the dead. The next day, he asked his wife to bring me a gift for "saving his life." I heartily thanked him but refused, telling him I'd done nothing out of the ordinary.

While I appreciated Mr. Hanson's expressions of gratitude, his life was never in my hands. Only God has the power of life and death. He is the one who keeps "our soul among the living" (Psalm 66:9) and offers us hope and comfort in our afflictions because His promise gives us life (Psalm 119:50).

God designed our bodies to be perfect, cells and systems working in unity. But here's the bad news: One day, sin entered the world. What was meant to last forever began to deteriorate. So God went a step further and redeemed us through the sacrifice of His Son, Jesus Christ. Now these bodies that get sick, break down, and just plain wear out are only our temporary homes. When we place ourselves in Jesus' hands, we are assured of one day receiving everlasting, imperishable, indestructible bodies (1 Corinthians 15:52-53).

Those are the capable hands I want to entrust with my life.

Prayer
Jesus, help me see beyond this life to the one You have planned for me. Touch my spirit and make me whole, as You always meant me to be. Amen.

For to set the mind on the flesh is death, but to set the
mind on the Spirit is life and peace.
— *Romans 8:6* —

God's Plans

For I know the plans I have for you," declares the
LORD, "plans to prosper you and not to harm you,
plans to give you hope and a future."
— Jeremiah 29:11 NIV —

Baseball practice ended. While the dads gathered to talk, some of the boys went to a corner of the church's large parking lot and threw the ball around. Ten-year-old Luke assumed his usual position as catcher. When the dads' group broke up, one of the men drove his SUV over to pick up his son.

Only he didn't see Luke squatting on the pavement.

The first time the vehicle ran over Luke, the other boys yelled and waved their arms. The dad, not understanding why they were so excited, backed up and ran over him again. This time, the man felt a bump and realized what must have happened. In a panic, he jumped out of the vehicle—and forgot to put it into park. By this point, the other dads had reached the scene. Luke's father grabbed the SUV's bumper trying to stop its momentum just as it rolled over his son for the third time.

But Luke was still alive.

They rushed him to the hospital, and doctors checked him over. Miraculously, Luke suffered no internal bleeding and only minor fractures. He returned home a few days later with scratches and lingering headaches but no other ill effects. His father's emotional description of seeing the SUV's huge tire flatten his son's head brought more than one strong man to tears.

Time and again, visitors told Luke that God must have special plans for him.

No doubt He did, but God has special plans for each of us, whether we've been run over by an SUV or not. We can discover those plans through prayer and join God in their implementation, giving us hope and the future He intends. Will it always be easy? No. Will our lives be marked by dazzling accomplishments, prominence, or fame? Maybe. Maybe not. We can't all be a Billy Graham, Tim Tebow, or Stephen Curtis Chapman. However, we can fulfill God's calling "with the strength God provides" (1 Peter 4:11 NIV), no matter what roles we play in life. Though it may not always look like it, God's plans surpass ours every time.

Prayer
Father, help me understand and find contentment in Your plans for me. Amen.

Better is one day in your courts than a thousand else-
where; I would rather be a doorkeeper in the house of
my God than dwell in the tents of the wicked.
        — Psalm 84:10 NIV —

Freedom

So Jesus said to the Jews who had believed him, "If
you abide in my word, you are truly my disciples, and
you will know the truth, and the truth will set you
free."
— John 8:31-32 —

My mother was "actively dying," as hospice nurses call it. In the midst of my grief, my vision suddenly blurred. Though I knew something had gone terribly wrong, I had no time to think about myself and pushed the notion to the back of my mind. When Mom passed away a few days later, I could no longer ignore the problem. As my husband drove me to the funeral home to make arrangements, I covered my right eye, and the cars coming at us on the busy city street simply . . . disappeared. Uh, oh.

The next day, my optometrist diagnosed a hole in my macula, the region at the back of my eye responsible for central vision. She sent me straight to a retinal doctor, who confirmed the diagnosis. He explained that the gel that holds my eye's shape had shrunk, as often happens with age. The fibers connecting the gel to my retina had released unevenly, and some had stuck, so to speak, to my macula. The result?

A macular hole that prevented my left eye from focusing clearly.

Fortunately, a new medication had recently become available that releases the fibers' traction on the macula, freeing the hole to close naturally. While I didn't relish the thought of an injection in my eye, it appealed more than surgery. It took months for my vision to recover, but I now see with little distortion.

Sometimes temptations take hold of us, just as the gel grabbed my macula, and before we realize it, they pull us in the wrong direction. Jesus has the cure—only He can set us free from the power of sin through His sacrifice on the cross. While we'll never be sinless, the apostle Paul said, "There is therefore now no condemnation for those who are in Christ Jesus. For the law of the Spirit of life has set you free in Christ Jesus from the law of sin and death" (Romans 8:1-2).

Just as the medication freed my macula to return to its normal position and take up its natural function again, so Jesus freed us from sin to return to God as children of righteousness. Now we can take up the work of helping others clearly see the path to freedom.

Prayer
Thank You, Jesus, for setting me free from the power of sin, something I could never do for myself. Amen.

So if the Son sets you free, you will be free indeed.
— John 8:36 —

The God of All Comfort

Even though I walk through the darkest valley, I will
fear no evil, for you are with me; your rod and your
staff, they comfort me.
— Psalm 23:4 NIV —

"What exactly is an arteriovenous malformation?" my friend Rhonda asked.

Accustomed to medical questions from family and friends, I went into nurse mode and explained that an arteriovenous malformation (AVM) is an abnormal knot of enlarged blood vessels where capillaries should be. "They're often found in the brain and can rupture, causing cerebral hemorrhage." Too late, I remembered Rhonda had recently visited a doctor for bouts of dizziness. I barely squeaked out, "Why do you ask?"

"That's what I have."

Just thirty-six years old and a homeschooling mother of five, Rhonda avidly researched the latest innovations for her condition. I accompanied her to neurologist appointments, discussed treatment options with her, and even drove her from our north Mississippi homes to consult a Chicago specialist. Doctors inserted tiny platinum coils to clot off the AVM and performed gamma knife surgery, in which they targeted the AVM with tightly focused beams of radiation. The first procedure left Rhonda with a mild stroke, and the second gave her an eight-month-long headache.

When I visited my friend in the hospital for an unrelated illness, she said, "I think I know why all this has happened to me." Rhonda patted the Bible lying on her lap. "It's so I can comfort others who are going through the same kind of thing."

To be honest, when I'm sick or afraid, all I want to do is hunker down and think about myself. As Rhonda knew, that's not what God calls us to do. God says, "I, even I, am he who comforts you" and promises that for the redeemed "gladness and joy will overtake them, and sorrow and sighing will flee away" (Isaiah 51:11-12 NIV). We can share that same promise with others who may be facing devastating illness. It's not easy, especially when we're in the middle of our own crises. Only when we acknowledge that God's unfailing love is our promised comfort (Psalm 119:76) can we share that comfort with others.

Prayer
Father, help me rise above my own troubles and comfort others as You have comforted me. Amen.

*Praise be to the God and Father of our Lord Jesus
Christ, the Father of compassion and the God of all
comfort, who comforts us in all our troubles, so that
we can comfort those in any trouble with the comfort
we ourselves receive from God.*
— 2 Corinthians 1:3-4 NIV —

No Mistake

Kate sat on the exam table and patted her swollen tummy, awaiting news on her unborn daughter's amniocentesis.

The obstetrician walked in, sat down, and opened her chart without looking at her. "Tests confirm the fetus has Down Syndrome. Your only option is to abort the pregnancy." The doctor's clinical tone brooked no argument.

For the briefest moment, the young mother considered his recommendation. Was she up to the task of raising a Down Syndrome child? Could she balance caring for a newborn with special needs and devoting time to her preschool son? Would their limited finances survive the medical bills? Then the shock wore off. This was her *baby* they were talking about, not a syndrome.

"I won't have an abortion," she said.

Four years later, Kate's little girl sat on a barstool at my kitchen counter, devouring a chocolate cupcake. I barely had time to swipe her mouth and hands with a washcloth before she slid from the stool and ran to play with her brother and my two sons. The child whose tests showed she had Down Syndrome had no genetic abnormalities.

Even the best of doctors armed with the most sophisticated medical technology do not know God's plans. If Kate had leaned on her own understanding (Proverbs 3:5) and listened to her fears, this bright little girl would never have been born. Even when the doctors' predictions come true, we can trust that God has a blueprint for each child's future (Psalm 139:16, Jeremiah 29:11, Psalm 40:5).

Every life is precious. God knew each of us—every cell in our bodies—before we came to be, and He knew what health challenges we would face. More importantly, He gave us the strength to face those challenges (Isaiah 41:10). We are His children, His creation, and that alone gives us hope.

Because God doesn't make mistakes.

Prayer
All-knowing God, keep me ever aware that You have eternal purposes for each life You created. Help me turn weaknesses into strengths and trust Your purposes for my life and for the lives of my family. Amen.

I praise you, for I am fearfully and wonderfully made.
Wonderful are your works; my soul knows it very
well.
— Psalm 139:14 —

The Best Medicine

A joyful heart is good medicine, but a crushed spirit
dries up the bones.
— Proverbs 17:22 —

My mother made an astonishing turnaround after having a shunt inserted into her brain to drain excess cerebrospinal fluid. Though she never completely regained mobility, I was overjoyed when her sense of humor returned.

One day, I drove her to a doctor's appointment and parked in an underground lot. After transferring her to a wheelchair, I stuck my head into the car to retrieve my purse and her records. When I straightened up, the wheelchair was freewheeling across the parking garage—with Mom in it! I sprinted over just in time to stop it from ramming an SUV. Horrified at what could have happened, I said, "I turned around, and you were gone!"

Without hesitation, she deadpanned, "I wait for no one."

I'm so glad God gave us laughter. How gloomy would the world be without it? And He did even more. Not only does that belly laugh lighten our moods, but the resulting release of endorphins and neuropeptides reduces pain and fights the effects of stress. Laughter potentially prevents even more serious illnesses. Our God thinks of everything.

But what about when the doctor diagnoses cancer or breaks the news that we have a chronic illness? While we won't laugh then, Christians have a source of joy even the most horrific news cannot eradicate, and that joy can sustain us through the worst of times to follow. King David told us he'd found the secret to this joy by setting "the LORD always before me; because he is at my right hand, I shall not be shaken" (Psalm 16:8). With our eyes on God, we can join the psalmist in proclaiming, "Those who sow in tears shall reap with shouts of joy!" (Psalm 126:5). We can't be happy all the time, but we can express our joy in the Lord.

So laugh. It's good medicine. And if you ask me, every doctor should carry a prescription pad for joy which includes titters, giggles, snickers, snorts, hoots, and guffaws. That should just about cure the ills of this world.

Prayer
When my heart is heavy, Lord, give me a good dose of laughter and fill me with Your healing joy. Amen.

Then our mouth was filled with laughter, and our
tongue with shouts of joy; then they said . . . The
LORD has done great things for us; we are glad.
 — Psalm 126:2-3 —

No Fear!

The LORD is my light and my salvation; whom shall I fear? The LORD is the stronghold of my life; of whom shall I be afraid?
— Psalm 27:1 —

An avid tennis player, our dentist seemed quite fit—until one day, a ball smacked him squarely in the sternum. Pain ricocheted through his chest and didn't dissipate with time. He tried to ignore it but finally decided it was more than a bruise. He went to the doctor, suspecting a fracture. Instead, he found out he had bone cancer. The blow didn't cause the cancer. It was already there, asymptomatic, lurking below the surface.

How do we take it when unexpected news blindsides us? Let's get real. If I received a distressing diagnosis—cancer, a degenerative neurological disease, kidney failure—fear and uncertainty would engulf me. My first response might be "Why did You let this happen, Lord?" In times like these, we're tempted to wonder if our beliefs about God are true.

Satan's lies sound loud and clear in tough moments. "A good God wouldn't do this to you. He doesn't love you. He doesn't care what happens to you." Satan can't rob us of our saving faith, but he does his best to steal our daily faith. Fear and doubt are some of his favorite weapons.

That's when we fight back with the sword of the spirit—God's Word (Ephesians 6:17). God is always good (Psalm 145:9): "The LORD is good to all, and his mercy is over all that he has made." God loves us (1 John 3:1): "See what kind of love the Father has given to us, that we should be called children of God." And He does care what happens to us (Psalm 34:4, 6): "I sought the LORD, and he answered me and delivered me from all my fears . . . This poor man cried, and the LORD heard him and saved him out of all his troubles."

Even King David had fears and doubts at times, but he revealed his total trust in God when he wrote, "You have said, 'Seek my face.' My heart says to you, 'Your face, LORD, do I seek'" (Psalm 27:8). We can turn to and trust the same God, without fear or doubt, no matter what the diagnosis.

Prayer
I praise You, Father, knowing You will give me courage to confront whatever I must and walk alongside me all the way. Amen.

I lay down and slept; I woke again, for the LORD *sustained me. I will not be afraid of many thousands of people who have set themselves against me all around.*
— *Psalm 3:5-6* —

My Advocate

*Even now my witness is in heaven; my advocate is on
high.*
— Job 16:19 NIV —

As my parents grew older, I often acted as their medical advocate. Dad suffered from a host of physical issues, and I struggled to keep his long list of medications straight, even with my nursing background. But I had no trouble remembering one drug. The cardiologist had told me, "Don't ever let anyone give him nitroglycerin while he's on this. The interaction would probably kill him."

Months later, my mom called to say Dad was struggling to breathe. I rushed him to the emergency room where he was admitted for congestive heart failure. I spent an exhausting day and night with him. At 6:00 the next morning, a young nurse crept into the room trying not to wake me and told Dad she had a medication for him. "What is it?" he asked. "A nitroglycerin patch," she replied. I popped off the couch like a jack-in-the-box and stopped her just before she applied it. I cringe to think what might have happened had I not been there to speak up.

As comforting as it is to have an advocate when we're sick, how much more reassuring is it to know we have not one but two advocates in the spiritual realm? While Jesus walked the earth, He promised believers He would not leave them defenseless. "And I will ask the Father, and he will give you another advocate to help you and be with you forever" (John 14:16 NIV). That advocate is "the Spirit of truth who goes out from the Father" (John 15:26 NIV). The Holy Spirit comforts us, helps us to pray, endows us with spiritual gifts—and convicts us of sin.

When I advocated for Dad, I protected him against those who might do wrong. What about when I'm the one who does wrong? Who will advocate for me? "But if anybody does sin, we have an advocate with the Father—Jesus Christ, the Righteous One" (1 John 2:1 NIV). What a relief to know I have the Holy Spirit standing beside me here on earth and Jesus interceding for me in heaven. That's advocacy at its best.

Prayer

Father, give me strength to avoid sin. When I do err, thank You for the convicting power of the Holy Spirit and my advocate on high, Jesus Christ, whose atoning sacrifice brings spiritual healing. Amen.

For there is one God and one mediator between God
and mankind, the man Christ Jesus.
— *1 Timothy 2:5 NIV* —

From Loss to Restoration

*I believe that I shall look upon the goodness of the
LORD in the land of the living! Wait for the LORD;
be strong, and let your heart take courage; wait for
the LORD!*
— Psalm 27:13-14 —

Helping my friend Sarita hunt for a wig wasn't what
either of us wanted to do with our day, but we made
an adventure of it. We visited several shops, tried
on wigs—some silly, some gorgeous—talked, and laughed.
She made her selection, and we celebrated with lunch at
an Italian restaurant. Cancer had attacked, but it wouldn't
defeat us.

For years, Sarita had suffered abdominal pain from endome-
triosis. When the pain became unbearable, she consented to
a hysterectomy, even though her family had just recovered
from a severe financial blow and she had no insurance. A
few days later, a doctor gave her the unwelcome news that
they'd found an ovarian cancer cell during surgery. One cell.

Torn over whether to proceed with more aggressive measures, Sarita thought of her daughters and opted for chemo.
Since she lacked insurance, friends drove her three hours
away for treatments despite excellent hospitals nearby. She

had an extreme reaction to one of the chemotherapy drugs and was in agony for days. Adhesions later required a second surgery, and she had a reaction to another medication while in the hospital. Her list of trials could fill a book.

Sarita experienced many losses—her "womanhood," her hair, financial security, and much of her independence—and she grieved each one. Yet she never lost heart. What was her secret? Yes, prayer covered every step, but Sarita had confidence that God would restore what "the locusts" had eaten—as He did for the Israelites (Joel 2:25), for Job (Job 42:12-13), and for Naomi (Ruth 4:15).

The kind of confidence Sarita radiated only comes through trust, and that level of trust comes only through faith that God will keep His promises. She agreed with King David that "some trust in chariots and some in horses, but we trust in the name of the LORD our God" (Psalm 20:7).

Today, Sarita is a healthy, beautiful woman with a successful job. God rewarded Sarita's trust and restored everything she had lost due to cancer.

Prayer
All praises to You, Lord, that I can have confidence in Your Word and Your goodness. I trust You with my future, whatever that may be. Amen.

I have always been mindful of your unfailing love and
have lived in reliance on your faithfulness.
— Psalm 26:3 NIV —

Who Are You Calling Old?

*Therefore we do not lose heart. Though outwardly we
are wasting away, yet inwardly we are being renewed
day by day.*
— 2 Corinthians 4:16 NIV —

Okay, so old age is not a disease, though many people treat it that way.

My mother-in-law turned ninety-nine this year and is as unique as her name. Fairsee creeps along with a walker, her vision has dimmed to the point she can barely read, and her once-acute hearing has diminished. Yet she wakes up singing each morning, keeps my husband and me up to date on world news, and is the first to get a joke. After Sunday morning worship service, a wave of people heads our way—not to say hi to me, mind you, but to talk to her.

It saddens me to see people patronize seniors—or worse, become impatient or ridicule them. I wish they realized how much older folks have to offer.

According to biblical accounts, God used many elderly people to accomplish His will. Moses embarked on a mission to lead his people to the promised land at the age of eighty (Exodus 7:7). Well into his eighties, Daniel received visions of the end times (Daniel 8–12). Sarah was ninety when she bore Isaac, making Abraham a daddy at one hundred (Genesis 17:17). No doubt their hair was gray and their joints creaked, but that didn't stop them from fulfilling God's purposes.

As we age and experience more health problems, sometimes serious ones, we may wonder if we no longer have value in God's eyes. We've raised our families, accomplished our goals, and run the race. What else is left to do? What else *can* we do?

Until three years ago, my mother-in-law lived on her own, cooked her own meals, and took no prescription medications. When her health declined and she had to move in with us, she could have decided she had nothing else to contribute. Instead, she prays for her loved ones, writes cards to relatives and church members, and delights her Sunday school class with ninety-nine years of insights. She tells everyone from the hairdresser to doctor's staff about Jesus. God is not through with her yet.

So don't despair. If you're still breathing, your mission is not complete. You will never outlive your usefulness to God.

Prayer
Thank You, Lord, for the elderly saints You've put in my life. Help me learn from them how to be a light for You. Amen.

[The righteous] will still bear fruit in old age, they will stay fresh and green, proclaiming, "The LORD is upright; he is my Rock, and there is no wickedness in him."
— Psalm 92:14-15 NIV —

Panic or Peace

For God is not a God of confusion but of peace.
— 1 Corinthians 14:33 —

Taking a vacation may have saved my life. One summer while I was gone, unprecedented rains struck our area and flooded the lower floor of the hospital where I worked, requiring evacuation of the newborn nursery. That was bad enough, but when flooding knocked out the air conditioners, doors opened to a killer. Unknown to anyone, the little-used backup system that kicked in harbored Legionella, the bacterium that causes Legionnaire's disease. By the time I returned to work, personnel and patients alike had come down with the deadly lung infection.

Though serious, Legionnaire's disease could not be spread by person-to-person contact, yet our supervisors insisted we use isolation techniques when caring for infected patients. So, we gowned and gloved, wore masks, and went about our business. Through the years, I'd nursed patients with gangrene, hepatitis, and a host of other infections and survived. While I thought it wise to take precautions, I saw this latest infectious agent as no different.

Leprosy, another nasty bacterium, has terrorized people since Old Testament times, eating away noses, ears, fingers, and toes. Sufferers had to live alone and shout, "Unclean, unclean," when anyone came near (Leviticus 13:45). The Black Plague killed upwards of 200 million people in the Middle Ages, and the flu pandemic of 1918 killed at least 50 million, one of them my grandmother's fiancé. MRSA, AIDS, Swine flu, SARS, Coronavirus—every few years, it seems a new superbug pops up, striking our most vulnerable and leaving fear and confusion in its wake. We don't know who to listen to, what to believe, or how to react.

I can see Satan now, jumping up and down with glee. He loves to use the same turmoil to prey on us, too. Fortunately, we have the means to guard ourselves—and not just with hand sanitizer and soap. When we wash in Jesus' cleansing blood, fortify with Scripture, and cover ourselves with prayer, we protect our hearts and minds from Satan's attacks. Then while everyone around us panics, we can experience the peace which "surpasses all understanding" (Philippians 4:7).

So, the next time another opportunistic organism (and that includes Satan) rears its ugly head, share the refuge that soothes fear and smooths away confusion. Maybe an outbreak of peace will infect the world.

Prayer
God of peace, I trust in You. No matter what happens around me, You will never change. Amen.

You keep him in perfect peace whose mind is stayed on
you, because he trusts in you.
— Isaiah 26:3 —

Miss Mae's Mission

*How beautiful on the mountains are the feet of those
who bring good news, who proclaim peace, who bring
good tidings, who proclaim salvation, who say to Zion,
"Your God reigns!"*
— *Isaiah 52:7 NIV* —

Urinary tract infections (UTIs) are no fun for anyone, but they can pose special problems for older
people. Some become confused or combative. Miss
Mae became an evangelist.

I visited this sweet saint from our church after she was
admitted to the hospital with both a severe UTI and an
electrolyte imbalance. When I arrived at her bedside, she
reached for my hand and said, "Do you know Jesus as your
Lord and Savior?" I raised an eyebrow at her husband. He
shrugged and said, "She's been asking everyone who comes
in that same question." Nurses, aids, lab technicians—even
friends from church—had to look into those blue eyes and
declare their salvation. Or lack thereof.

Oh, that we would always be so bold in proclaiming our
faith in Jesus Christ! Miss Mae broadcast the gospel from
her hospital bed, bringing others into the kingdom of light
(Colossians 1:12). What better way to show love than to

tell those we come into contact with about Jesus' sacrifice and offer them the gift of spending eternity in heaven with Him? And we don't have to "walk the mountains"—or the hospital corridors—to do it.

Yet how often do we miss opportunities to share the good news? We fear people will think us strange or that we won't know the right words to say when all we really have to do is show them our love for the Lord. God's concern extends to all those within our reach (2 Peter 3:9), and our salvation is not something God wants us to hide. That's why He has already put a "new song" of praise into our mouths, and "many will see and fear the LORD and put their trust in him" (Psalm 40:3 NIV).

We can become evangelists wherever we find ourselves. Even a hospital bed.

Prayer
Jesus, forgive me for the times I've squandered the openings You gave me to tell others about You. Please make me tender toward the lost and bold in sharing Your gospel of saving grace. Amen.

*I do not seal my lips, L*ORD*, as you know. I do not
hide your righteousness in my heart; I speak of your
faithfulness and your saving help.*
— Psalm 40:9-10 NIV —

All Means All

In addition to having normal pressure hydrocephalus, my mother also developed another mouthful-of-a-condition known as neurocardiogenic syncope. Her neurologist suspected it when we told him she'd passed out twice while she stood in the kitchen cooking dinner. Her cardiologist confirmed the diagnosis by ordering a tilt table test.

Neurocardiogenic syncope occurs when the part of the nervous system that controls heart rate and blood pressure malfunctions in response to a trigger. In Mom's case, standing for a long time triggered her fainting spells. Blood pooled in her legs, and her body couldn't compensate. When her heart rate and blood pressure dropped, it was lights out for her. The cardiologist inserted a pacemaker, and she never passed out again.

When our systems work together, our bodies run smoothly. But one little thing out of whack can play havoc. So it is in our relationship with God. Three of the four gospels report Jesus' response when asked to name the greatest commandment (Matthew 22:37, Mark 12:30, Luke 10:27). He didn't say just, "Love God." He said to use every part of our being—heart, soul, and mind—holding nothing back. Only when we let our love for God rule everything—our thoughts, words, and actions—will our spiritual health be sound.

This seems like an impossible task in the world we live in. It is—if we try to do it on our own. In fact, completely loving God requires heart surgery according to Deuteronomy 30:6: "And the LORD your God will circumcise your heart . . . so that you will love the LORD your God with all your heart and with all your soul, that you may live."

A pacemaker doesn't take over the function of the heart. It just stimulates it to beat properly when it's out of rhythm. However, God does want to take over our hearts—and I can't imagine our lives running any more smoothly than when we're in rhythm with Him.

Prayer
Jesus, help me daily to obey the most important commandment, to love God with all my heart, soul, and mind, as You did. Amen.

*"Only be very careful to observe the commandment
and the law, . . . to love the LORD your God, and to
walk in all his ways and to keep his commandments
and to cling to him and to serve him with all your
heart and with all your soul."*
— *Joshua 22:5* —

One Tiny Seed

He does not deal with us according to our sins, nor re-
pay us according to our iniquities. For as high as the
heavens are above the earth, so great is his steadfast
love toward those who fear him.
— *Psalm 103:10-11* —

A harmless act. Something most of us did as children. Now an eight-year-old fought for his life. I gathered with other nursing students around the little boy's bed to hear his story. One bright spring day, he plucked a dandelion puffball and blew it, sending tiny parachutes flying on the breeze. When he inhaled to blow again, he aspirated one of the feathery seeds. In the dark, moist environment of his lung, the seed germinated. Irritation led to an abscess, causing the child to fall seriously ill. Doctors performed a bronchoscopy, but despite powerful antibiotics, infection raged.

All because of one tiny seed.

The child was not responsible for what happened to him. But how many times do we allow things to enter our lives that are not pleasing to God, that end up causing us great harm? At first, we tell ourselves it's no big deal, just a minor indiscretion. Over time, it becomes embedded in our routine, something we don't even think about—until one day, we find ourselves in serious trouble.

Oftentimes, that's how sin starts. It settles into our lives, just as the seed settled into the child's lung. The longer it remains, unaddressed, the more entrenched the "infection" becomes. Fortunately, God put a treatment plan in place long ago. The simple but effective prescription is found in 1 John 1:9: "If we confess our sins, he is faithful and just to forgive us our sins and to cleanse us from all unrighteousness."

The apostle Paul said God will also help us practice preventive medicine so we can avoid the pain sin brings altogether. "God is faithful, and he will not let you be tempted beyond your ability, but with the temptation he will also provide the way of escape, that you may be able to endure it" (1 Corinthians 10:13). That's the kind of health plan I like!

Sin so easily enters our lives. Only by turning to God in repentance can we stop it from taking root. Because it's surprising what one tiny seed can do.

Prayer
Lord, show me any areas of my life where sin has taken hold and give me the wisdom and strength to uproot it. Amen.

Search me, O God, and know my heart! Try me and know my thoughts! And see if there be any grievous way in me, and lead me in the way everlasting!
— *Psalm 139:23-24* —

Nothing but the Word

*I have hidden your word in my heart that I might not
sin against you.*
— *Psalm 119:11 NIV* —

Miss Ruth was in her eighties and already suffered from heart disease when I first knew her. She entered our writers group meetings on a walker and often leaned forward on the table to catch her breath. To my surprise, her voice was always as clear and strong as a drill sergeant's, her commanding yet loving demeanor evidence of years spent teaching school.

One day, she told our group a story about her childhood. On Saturdays, while other neighborhood children played outside, Ruth's mother made her sit at the kitchen table and memorize Scripture. Ruth heard her friends' laughter through the open window, but she had to stay with the task each week until she could quote the verses back to her mother. Though she sometimes resented not being able to go outside and play, Ruth was thankful her mother disciplined her to learn God's Word. She said those verses came to mind later in life just when she needed them most.

Reading the Bible opens our eyes to God's truth, but the day may come when we don't have access to Scripture. What then? No one can take away the verses we've memorized over the years. The Bible itself says God's Word softens our hearts (Jeremiah 23:29), guides us (Psalm 119:105), instructs us (2 Timothy 3:16), and so much more. We have no more powerful weapon, whether offensive or defensive, in the battle for our souls. But it takes diligence and effort to commit Scripture to memory.

After telling her story, Miss Ruth challenged us to learn a verse every week over the next twelve months. I was happy to report a year later that I had memorized not 52 but 104 verses. Miss Ruth beamed as though I were her best student.

Shortly thereafter, her health worsened, and she became homebound. I was only able to keep up with her through email. Yet her enthusiasm for the written word, especially God's Word, never waned. The Scriptures sustained and comforted her during days when she could do nothing but recite the verses she'd learned as a child. How glad I am that I accepted her challenge to hide God's Word in my heart, too.

Prayer
Lord, thank You for the comfort Your Word brings in my darkest moments. Speak to me through Scripture and help me call verses to mind when I need them. Amen.

*I remember, LORD, your ancient laws, and I find
comfort in them.*
— Psalm 119:52 NIV —

Preparing for the Unexpected

*"Watch therefore, for you know neither the day nor
the hour."*
— *Matthew 25:13* —

It started out like an intestinal virus, not my favorite way to spend Labor Day. The vomiting and diarrhea subsided around 2 a.m., and I spent the next morning in bed with a low-grade fever—my usual *modus operandi* after a stomach bug. As the day wore on, my fever rose. The soreness in my abdomen that I'd assumed was from heaving the night before migrated to the right lower quadrant. I had little pain but figured if nothing else, I was probably dehydrated. So off to the hospital we went.

After blood work and a CT scan, the ER physician diagnosed appendicitis. What? I didn't have time for surgery. My mom required twenty-four-hour care. Even though we hired caregivers, I went to her house twice daily to give injections and put her to bed. At the time, she also had a PICC line through which she was receiving nutritional supplements and antibiotics, which I administered. My dad needed me in a myriad of ways, and the caregivers depended on me to coordinate everything. I was indispensable!

God said otherwise. Surgery revealed a perforated appendix. Sicker than I realized, I spent a week in the hospital and several more weeks recuperating while friends and family took over caregiving responsibilities. I wasn't as indispensable as I thought.

Illness and accidents assail us without warning. We can't prepare for them. But we can prepare our hearts for Jesus. He could return or call us home at any moment, and like the foolish virgins in Matthew 25 (vv. 1-13), we might find ourselves locked out if we aren't ready.

While I didn't expect surgery, I do know what God expects. I'm accountable for ensuring my own spiritual condition. No one else can do it for me. Accepting Jesus' gift of salvation is essential (Romans 10:9-10), but preparation also involves cultivating a personal relationship with my Lord and Master. In addition, I'm responsible for developing and using the gifts God has given me to further His kingdom (Matthew 25:14-30).

I'm glad I'll never have to face appendicitis again, but that doesn't mean another emergency won't sideline me. Fortunately, my eternal preparations don't include surprises.

Prayer
Jesus, thank You for the assurance that I have salvation in You and that nothing will be able to separate me from Your love (Romans 8:39). Amen.

Therefore you also must be ready, for the Son of Man
is coming at an hour you do not expect.
— *Matthew 24:44* —

Bitter Wounds

But you, Sovereign LORD, help me for your name's sake; out of the goodness of your love, deliver me. For I am poor and needy, and my heart is wounded within me.
— Psalm 109:21-22 NIV —

Whenever I visited my mother at the skilled nursing facility, I passed Marie scooting herself down the hall in a wheelchair. A mere wisp of a woman, she would flash the sweetest smile and greet me with pleasant, though sometimes incomprehensible, sentiments.

One day, I found her sitting in her wheelchair weeping inconsolably. "What's wrong, Marie?" I asked, leaning over her.

She grabbed my arm and babbled that "they" took away her baby. The nurses often gave female patients baby dolls to cuddle when they were agitated. Was Marie referring to an offense that happened at the facility? Or did dementia twist her memories? Perhaps my imagination took flight, but Marie's outburst seemed to stem from something deeper. I tried to comfort her, but she would have none of it. Finally, I had to ease my hand from her grasp and turn her over to an aide so I could take my mother to a doctor's appointment.

I treated some serious wounds in my nursing career, but wounds of the heart originate from deep within, where neither medicine nor surgery can reach.

We've all been wronged at one time or another, sometimes profoundly. While we may have a right to feel anger, allowing that anger to turn into bitterness that infects our hearts can create a wound that never heals. When we practice preventive medicine, we follow Paul's admonition to "get rid of all bitterness, rage and anger, brawling and slander, along with every form of malice" (Ephesians 4:31 NIV). Right away. Before it makes us sick at heart.

I admit that I have failed at times to stop bitterness from taking root. What happens when we don't take the defensive measures Paul described? Psalm 32:5 outlines a two-step plan involving our confession and God's forgiveness. Then we can cry out with the psalmist, "Create in me a clean heart, O God, and renew a right spirit within me" (Psalm 51:10). God's medicine may not always be pleasant, but it can rid us of the underlying cause of our deep wounds and allow restoration to take place.

Prayer
Father, You have the only cure for bitterness. Give me humility and strength to apply it to my heart. Amen.

Is there no balm in Gilead? Is there no physician there? Why then is there no healing for the wound of my people?
— Jeremiah 8:22 NIV —

Bubbling Over with Joy

*Sing for joy, O heavens, and exult, O earth; break
forth, O mountains, into singing! For the LORD has
comforted his people and will have compassion on his
afflicted.*
— Isaiah 49:13 —

Using a cane, Donald walks haltingly into the sanctuary on Sunday mornings. His speech is slow and sometimes difficult to understand. But I love to watch him during worship. He raises his hands at the mention of Jesus' sacrifice, wipes away tears with a red handkerchief, and shouts with delight in the middle of the sermon. Rapture, love, ecstasy, bliss—all dance across Donald's face. But most of all, I see joy.

Donald's present state stems from a far-from-joyful experience in 1988. One night, while driving back to the New Jersey naval base where he was stationed, a deer darted in front of him. His truck flipped, and he was thrown through the windshield. An EMT thought he was dead at the scene. Then he detected a faint pulse. The ambulance rushed Donald to the closest hospital, but doctors gave his parents no hope and advised them multiple times to remove their son from the ventilator. However, God wasn't finished with him. After three months in a coma, he awoke!

Many things will always be hard for Donald, but he draws strength from a source most people don't associate with joy. Nehemiah understood. When the Israelites wept after being convicted of sin during a reading of God's Word, Nehemiah said, "And do not be grieved, for the joy of the LORD is your strength" (Nehemiah 8:8-10).

Happiness depends on our circumstances, but true joy comes from deep inside—bought by Jesus, placed there by a loving God, and nurtured by the Holy Spirit. Joy cannot be crushed by what goes on around us. When the doctor delivers the feared diagnosis, our loved one deteriorates before our eyes, or pain rules our days and nights, only the joy of the Lord gives us strength to help us bear the adversity. No one—and no situation—will take that joy away from us (John 16:22).

Donald celebrates that God chose to keep him on this earth a while longer. Rather than feel anger or resentment at his disabilities, he bubbles over with joy. His infectious display touches the lives of so many others as he worships his Savior with abandon.

Prayer
Jesus, I praise You even when life is hard because I know You care for me. Amen.

Let those who delight in my righteousness shout for joy
and be glad and say evermore, "Great is the LORD,
who delights in the welfare of his servant!"
— *Psalm 35:27* —

A Sure Foundation

So this is what the Sovereign LORD *says: "See, I lay
a stone in Zion, a tested stone, a precious cornerstone
for a sure foundation; the one who relies on it will
never be stricken with panic."*
— Isaiah 28:16 NIV —

I'd never considered osteoporosis all that serious, much less life threatening, until a relative developed a severe case. Always small-framed, her bones became more brittle as she grew older, and fractures resulted. Once, she simply stepped off a curb and broke her ankle. In another instance, she flipped out a t-shirt while folding clothes and fractured a wrist. Pain became her constant companion.

Others have had similar experiences. One woman said she could break a bone just by brushing her hair. Otherwise healthy people, both women and men, undergo bone loss as they age because the foundation of their skeletons—calcium—leaches from bones faster than it is replaced. As a result, bones begin to thin, becoming more and more porous and fragile, and resulting fractures can even lead to death. All from lack of a mineral commonly found in stone.

Foundation is important. Construction workers know that. They dig footings and pour concrete, carefully laying strong groundwork so the infrastructure doesn't shift and cause problems later. In the same way, our skeletons provide the infrastructure for our bodies, and calcium supplies the strength. A strong foundation is as essential in our spiritual lives as in the physical, and it matters what we lay as our groundwork. If we don't have a sure underpinning, we will fall—with disastrous consequences.

Throughout the Bible, God refers to Jesus Christ as the cornerstone, "and the one who trusts in him will never be put to shame" (1 Peter 2:6 NIV). Jesus provides the only solid foundation on which we can depend. With Him as our bedrock, the storms of life cannot destroy us. King David asked, "When the foundations are being destroyed, what can the righteous do?" (Psalm 11:3 NIV). With Jesus, we need not worry—He will always stand firm.

Prayer
Jesus, I trust You with my life. No matter what illness comes my way, I can weather it with You as my foundation. Amen.

*"Therefore everyone who hears these words of mine
and puts them into practice is like a wise man who
built his house on the rock. The rain came down, the
streams rose, and the winds blew and beat against
that house; yet it did not fall, because it had its foundation on the rock."*
— Matthew 7:24-25 NIV —

By Whatever Means

*To the weak I became weak, to win the weak. I have
become all things to all people so that by all possible
means I might save some.*
— *1 Corinthians 9:22 NIV* —

Linda, the director of an equine therapy program where
my son volunteered, had witnessed many breakthroughs
in the use of horses to treat the mentally and physically challenged. One case that particularly touched her in-
volved a severely autistic preschooler who could not connect
with the world around him. Collin's actions were robotic, he
rarely spoke, and he couldn't tolerate being touched. At the
start, he screamed whenever volunteers set him atop Buck,
a gentle quarter horse. Linda found she could calm him by
singing children's Sunday school songs. "Jesus Loves Me"
was his favorite.

Months went by with little improvement. After almost a
year, Linda considered telling Collin's mother there was
nothing more she could do. Then one day, she took him
along a new outdoor sensory trail.

As Linda led Buck back into the arena, Collin inexplicably
sat up and made eye contact with her for the first time.
He looked at the horse he rode and other things in the

arena as if he'd never seen them before. When Linda lifted Collin from the saddle, she placed him in his mother's arms where he snuggled for an hour while his mother cried with joy. Later, after Collin left, his mom called Linda's phone. "Listen!" she said. In the background, Linda could hear a tiny voice singing, "Jesus loves me, this I know . . ."

God still performs miracles—whether He works through doctors, nurses, therapists, or horses. In the same way, He will use whatever means necessary to touch our hearts. The Holy Spirit may speak through a preacher, a friend, an evangelist—or an illness. Then it's up to us to respond to the gift of salvation (Ephesians 2:8-9, Revelation 22:17). Without it, we walk around like robots and see only the temporal world, not realizing we are missing the eternal.

When we awaken to the sin in our lives and comprehend that Jesus is the only way to salvation, we can choose to become a child of God through repentance and faith. That is the greatest miracle of healing we can ever hope to experience.

Prayer
Jesus, I can't thank You enough for Your sacrifice and gift of eternal salvation. I look forward to the glorious day when I will stand in Your presence—healthy, healed, and whole. Amen.

So we fix our eyes not on what is seen, but on what is unseen, since what is seen is temporary, but what is unseen is eternal.
— *2 Corinthians 4:18 NIV* —

Bless the LORD, O my soul,
and all that is within me,
bless his holy name!
Bless the LORD, O my soul,
and forget not all his benefits,
who forgives all your iniquity,
who heals all your diseases,
who redeems your life from the pit,
who crowns you with steadfast love and mercy.

— Psalm 103:1-4 —

About the Author

Tracy Crump loves to delve into God's Word and has published close to one hundred devotions in magazines such as *Upper Room*, *Light from the Word*, *Quiet Hour*, and *Secret Place* as well as Guideposts books *All God's Creatures* and *One-Minute Devotions*. Thirty of her stories have appeared in anthologies, most in Chicken Soup for the Soul® books. She has published numerous articles in magazines such as *Focus on the Family*, *ParentLife*, *Mature Living*, and *Woman's World*. She contributed articles to three newspapers and wrote a column for *Southern Writers Magazine* for four years.

In 2008, Tracy co-founded Write Life Workshops. She conducts workshops and webinars that encourage others to "Write Better, Write Now!" Her course on writing for Chicken Soup for the Soul is one of Serious Writer Academy's top sellers. She edits The Write Life, a free e-newsletter for writers that has inspired many to move forward with their writing. Her love of teaching also takes her to conferences where she helps writers hone their craft. She is a freelance editor and works as a proof-reader for *Farmers' Almanac*. One book she edited received a coveted star review from *Publishers Weekly*.

Tracy wanted to be a nurse from the time she was ten years old. She worked in intensive care at a large metropolitan hospital and acted as primary caregiver for her parents for six years. Now she helps care for her 99-year-old mother-in-law. In addition, she walked alongside several friends experiencing harrowing health crises.

Tracy lives in north Mississippi with Stan, her husband of more than forty years. They have two sons and four adorable grandchildren, and she believes "Grandma" is the most beautiful word in the English language.

Websites: TracyCrump.com or WriteLifeWorkshops.com

Facebook: facebook.com/AuthorTracyCrump

Twitter: twitter.com/TracyCrumpWrite

LinkedIn: linkedin.com/in/tracycrump

Thank you from CrossLink Publishing

We appreciate your support of quality faith-based books. If you enjoyed this book would you consider sharing it with others?

- Mention the book on Facebook, Twitter, Pinterest, or your blog.

- Recommend this book to your small group, book club, or work colleagues.

- Pick up a copy for someone you know who would be encouraged by this book.

- Write a review on Amazon.com, Goodreads.com, or BarnesandNoble.com.

- To learn about our latest releases, check out the **Coming Soon** section of our website: CrossLinkPublishing.com

Printed in the United States
By Bookmasters